Isobel

Thank you so much for coming to my event. I appreciate the support. Make recipes and tag @dontyoudairy—

XOXO
Bobbie Cheri

Don't You Dairy
50 Dairy-Free & Delicious Recipes

Bobbie Cheri Gobert

EDITORS

Ezra Thorne
Recipes
Shannon Luders-Manuel
Acknowledgements,
Introduction, and
Must Haves
Ezra Thorne
Photography
Miles Stancil
Author photo
Myshell Tabu
Book design

Library of Congress Control Number
2019908870

ACKNOWLEDGEMENTS

I would like to dedicate this book to my mom, my husband, and my tribe. These people, whom I love so much, are the reasons why I am writing this book.

My mother started her professional culinary career after my sister and I were grown. She went to school and learned the skills to match her natural talent for cooking. My mom, Banana Butt (that's what I call my grandma), my Granny (RIP), my Auntie Dottie, and my Grandma Ruthie were all great cooks. Out of all the grandkids, I was the one with the natural talent in the kitchen. I'm sorry guys, but you all know this statement is true. #fightme. Growing up I watched my mom literally make everything from scratch. The only time we ate fast food was when I spent the night over at a friend's house. She's taught me that it's never too late to follow your dreams and it's not how you start but how you finish.

My husband has so much determination and ambition. He chose to make something of his life despite the cards he was dealt. He went from the Air Force to the music industry, to video game publishing, and now he is in tech. He taught himself how to code in six months and landed himself an incredible job that he loves. Seeing him so excited about learning encourages me so much. Every day I am amazed by him and how much he has accomplished. After moving on from my last career, I found myself really depressed. It's mostly attributed to my fibromyalgia, which I talk about later on, but I was also in a fragile state and felt lost. My husband has been so supportive while I've been on this journey to fulfill my purpose. He told me to find what I'm really passionate about and give it everything I've got. With his love and paycheck, *cues Destiny's Child's "Bills Bills Bills"*, that is exactly what I'm doing.

My tribe is amazing. Imagine like 50 women (this is not an exaggerated number) daily encouraging you, cheering you on, and supporting you. Sometimes people see things in us that we don't see in ourselves because we are so focused on our shortcomings. More times than not, this keeps us from moving forward. These super dope women, along with my besties, played a huge role in me not giving up.

God placed the idea to write this cookbook in my heart years ago, and with the help of my mom, my husband, and my tribe, I finally got the courage to see it through.

CONTENTS

INTRODUCTION

Why No Dairy?

It all started when I was diagnosed with fibromyalgia years ago. For those who are unfamiliar with the term, in a nutshell it is your nerves overacting. They send signals to your brain that there is pain or trauma when there is none. It's a chronic illness and literally all in my head. The process to get diagnosed was probably the hardest part for me. My fibromyalgia was diagnosed by the process of elimination. I got tested for everything, and when those things were ruled out, they diagnosed me with fibromyalgia. You can imagine how frustrating it can be when you are telling your doctor your arm is on fire or you need a body scan because you believe that your bones are shrinking, and the costs of all these tests can be very expensive. I felt like a kid trying to convince a parent that she saw a ghost. Thankfully my doctor was great and immediately started testing to get to the bottom of this unfamiliar pain.

Fibromyalgia is said to be triggered by an infection or injury. For me, it was a kidney infection. After the diagnosis, I decided I was not going to be doped up on meds with a list of side effects longer than my grocery list. My doctor gave me recommendations on how to cope and minimize what I call "flare ups." Removing dairy from my diet was one of the recommendations. It's been over six years and I am coping so much better since I eliminated dairy from my diet.

Growing up I was never a big milk drinker, but I loved cheese, ice cream, cakes and pies. After the diagnosis I felt like my love affair with food was about to be over. I knew this new lifestyle was going to be challenging, but I was committed—to the point of annoyance for my friends—to live dairy free. I go out of my way to read every ingredient in everything I eat. Did you know BBQ Lays chips have milk in them? Well, they do. I was surprised at some of the products that contained dairy. Like, full-on shock. I realized the only way to ensure I don't consume dairy was to cook at home and try to stay away from packaged and processed foods.

Why a Cookbook?

Coming from a family of cooks, food has always been a huge part of who I am. It's a way for me to show my love to my family and friends. I am known for impromptu gatherings at my house, just so I can cook for them. My husband often says he's never seen anyone get so excited when talking about food. Being able to take a bunch of ingredients and make something that people love is amazing. I have something to offer this world that doesn't require Lactaid ... and, if I must say so myself, it is pretty amazing!

There are tons of restaurants that cater to the gluten-free as well as the vegan. If I can be honest, I felt left out. I love meat. I just don't want it cooked with butter. I found myself going out less because I was kind of being forced to eat vegan to ensure that I wasn't consuming dairy unknowingly. I personally don't want to eat faux meat. Also, going out to eat became a whole ordeal. If I was going out to eat with friends, I would try to call the restaurant ahead of time to see what I could eat. There is nothing worse than making a fuss or holding up the ordering process so the waiter can go ask the chef if something was cooked with dairy. I find that when speaking to waiters about food issues, they will only give you surface-level solutions.

For example, if I see a sandwich on the menu, he will suggest that I can eat it if I remove the cheese. He does not know if the bread itself contains butter, milk, or cream. It is my responsibility to do my own research. I cannot rely on the waiter to assure me of things they do not know.

I think it's important to understand that everyone has different lifestyles and convictions when it comes to eating, but there is room for all of us at the dinner table. Some people don't want to eat meat or drink milk because they want their body to be as clean and healthy as possible. That doesn't mean they have a problem with wearing fur. Let people live their best life. *Cues Lil Duval's song "Smile."* What's funny is I've had people try to embarrass me while eating something by saying, "Oh I thought you didn't eat dairy. You seem so firm about it." When I tell them that I am firm on it, they say, "Well you're eating mayo." This is a teachable but funny moment for people trying to poke holes in my dairy-free movement. I inform them that mayo has eggs in it and eggs are from a chicken. Hopefully people will read this cookbook and be enlightened as well as inspired.

What Do I Know?

In a nutshell, I know how to make delicious food. I've been cooking since I was young. Being able to whip something up, for myself and my sister, kept us from starving when my mother was on her "every man for himself" antics after school. I never followed recipes and just cooked by taste. My mom always said, "When you make a dish, write it down so it tastes the same every time." Did I listen? Nope. This is part of why it has taken me some time to complete this book; I had to literally start from scratch. Note to self: #listentomom.

As I share with you the dishes I love, you will discover that a life without dairy is worth living. I hope you enjoy them as much as I do!

MY MUST-HAVES

Dairy Substitutions

When you are substituting dairy, you can't just replace it with something non-dairy. Measurements may need to be changed, and, most importantly, you have to find the right products so the taste isn't compromised. Some vegan cheeses I give two thumbs all the way down. I made the mistake of assuming that since I liked one type of cheese alternative from a brand, all of them would taste good. Daiya's Pepperjack and Mozzarella style shreds are good, the cheddar is not. Let us not be fooled!

It has taken me some time, but I found the best dairy substitutions that don't make you miss dairy. These are the brands I prefer to use for my recipes. Using other dairy substitutions that I do not mention is not recommended, as they may alter the taste of the dish.

1. **Earth Balance or Smart Balance -** Butter alternative.
2. **Trader Joe's Vegan Cream Cheese -** Cream cheese alternative.
3. **Tofutti Better Than Sour Cream -** Sour cream alternative.
4. **Simple Truth Unsweetened Almond Milk -** Milk alternative.
5. **Daiya Mozzarella Style Shreds -** Cheese alternative.
6. **Daiya Pepperjack Style Shreds -** Cheese alternative.
7. **Follow Your Heart Provolone Style Slices -** Cheese alternative.
8. **Follow Your Heart Smoked Gouda Style Slices -** Cheese alternative.
9. **Follow Your Heart Parmesan Style Shredded Cheese -** Cheese alternative.
10. **Follow Your Heart Vegan Ranch Dressing -** Ranch dressing alternative.

DON'T BE SALTY

Spice Blends, Sauces, and Dressings

There are plenty of times in life when we get boxed into the same tastes over and over again. However, in order to keep our dishes fresh, there are many spices that can be created and used along with salt or as a salt substitute that will keep us excited about the foods we eat. I really do believe it's all about "the sauce," both literally and figuratively. You can always think outside the box in order to make something new and exciting, and you don't always have to be limited to dry seasonings. While some of us prefer our dry spice mixes, there are some foods that we are not a fan of unless it's drenched in something or there is something to dip it in.

BOBBIE'S
HOUSE MIX

This is the spice mix I use the most. You may want to double the recipe if you cook often.

- 2 tablespoons Cajun seasoning
- 2 tablespoons salt
- 2 tablespoons black pepper
- 1/4 cup onion powder
- 1/4 cup garlic powder
- 2 tablespoons paprika

DIRECTIONS
1. In an airtight container with a lid, combine all ingredients and shake well.

TIP
Store in your cupboard. Discard after 6 months.

BLACKENED
SPICE

This mix is perfect for fish, chicken, and shrimp.

- 2 tablespoons sweet or plain paprika
- 1 1/2 tablespoons salt
- 2 teaspoons onion powder
- 2 teaspoons garlic powder
- 1/2 teaspoon cayenne pepper
- 2 teaspoons black pepper
- 1 teaspoon dried thyme
- 1 teaspoon dried oregano

DIRECTIONS
1. In an airtight container with a lid, combine all ingredients and shake well.

TIP
Store in your cupboard. Discard after 6 months.

SEASONED
FLOUR

This mix can be used as a primary taste to make gravy, cream sauces, and for frying chicken.

- 2 cups all purpose flour
- 1 tablespoon Cajun seasoning
- 1 tablespoon salt
- 1 tablespoon onion powder
- 1 tablespoon garlic powder
- 1 tablespoon sweet or plain paprika
- 2 teaspoons black pepper
- 1 teaspoon Ac'cent flavor enhancer

DIRECTIONS
1. In an airtight container with a lid, combine all ingredients and shake well.

TIP
Store in your cupboard. Discard after 3 months.

RED PEPPER
REMOULADE

This is great for use as a dipping sauce for meat and veggies, or a spread on sandwiches.

- 1 (12 ounce) jar of fire roasted red peppers, drained
- 1/2 cup Best Foods mayo
- 1/2 teaspoon fresh lemon juice
- 1 teaspoon minced garlic
- 1/4 teaspoon black pepper
- 1/4 teaspoon cayenne pepper
- 1/4 teaspoon salt
- 1 tablespoon parsley

DIRECTIONS
1. In a blender or NutriBullet, blend all ingredients together and serve.

TIP
Store in refrigerator in a glass jar or plastic airtight container with a lid. Discard after 2 weeks.

CAESAR
DRESSING

Add this dressing on top of Romaine lettuce with croutons and your favorite grilled meat.

- 1 cup Best Foods mayo
- 2 tablespoons fresh lemon juice
- 1 teaspoon stone ground mustard
- 1 teaspoon Worcestershire sauce
- 2 1/2 teaspoons anchovy paste
- 1 teaspoon minced garlic
- 1/2 teaspoon black pepper
- 1/4 cup Follow Your Heart parmesan cheese

DIRECTIONS
1. In a mixing bowl, combine all ingredients with a whisk.

TIP
Store in refrigerator in a glass jar or plastic airtight container with a lid. Discard after 2 weeks.

Chimichurri
SAUCE

This sauce tastes amazing on any sandwich or panini.

- 1/2 cup McCormicks dry chimichurri seasoning
- 1 cup olive oil
- 2 teaspoons onion powder
- 2 teaspoons ground sweet basil
- 1 teaspoon salt
- 2 teaspoons honey
- 1 tablespoon stone ground mustard

DIRECTIONS
1. In a mixing bowl, combine all ingredients with a spatula.

TIP
Store in refrigerator in a glass jar or plastic airtight container with a lid. Discard after 2 weeks.

SWEET & TANGY
VINAIGRETTE

Dress up any salad with this dressing.

- 2/3 cup Canola oil
- 1/4 cup red wine vinegar
- 1 garlic clove, crushed
- 1 teaspoon stone ground mustard
- 2 teaspoons honey
- 1/4 teaspoon salt
- 1/2 teaspoon onion powder
- 1/2 teaspoon sweet or plain paprika
- 1/4 teaspoon black pepper
- 1/4 teaspoon crushed red pepper

DIRECTIONS
1. In a mixing bowl, combine all ingredients with a spatula.

TIP
Store in refrigerator in a glass jar or plastic airtight container with a lid. Shake well before each use. Discard after 3 weeks.

SPECIAL
SAUCE

Use this sauce on your burger or sandwich for a slight kick.

- 1/4 cup Best Foods mayo
- 2 teaspoons chopped Hot & Sweet jalapeños
- 1 teaspoon picked relish
- 1 1/2 teaspoons ketchup
- Pinch of salt
- 1 teaspoon yellow mustard
- 1/4 teaspoon smoked paprika
- 1/4 teaspoon garlic powder
- 1/4 teaspoon onion powder

DIRECTIONS
1. In a mixing bowl, combine all ingredients with a whisk.

TIP
Store in the refrigerator in a glass jar or plastic airtight container with a lid. Discard after 2 weeks.

IT'S ALL
GRAVY

Smother any meat or poultry with this gravy, or serve it over mashed potatoes or rice.

- 2 tablespoons Canola oil
- 1/4 cup seasoned flour (see page 13 for recipe)
- 1 1/4 cups water
- 1 teaspoon chicken bouillon powder

DIRECTIONS
1. In a saucepan, heat oil on high heat.
2. Add seasoned flour and occasionally stir 5 minutes.
3. Using a whisk, stir in water a little at a time to avoid lumps.
4. Add chicken bouillon powder and cook 2 to 3 minutes. Stir occasionally with a spoon.
5. Serve over rice or your favorite meat.

TIP
Store in refrigerator in an airtight container with a lid. To reheat, place in saucepan on medium high heat and add a little water to thin out. Discard after 1 week.

CREAM OF MUSHROOM
SAUCE

This sauce is used in other recipes in the cookbook, but can be served by itself on top of rice.

- 1 (8 ounce) pack mushrooms, finely chopped
- 1 tablespoon Canola oil
- 2 teaspoons Bobbie's house mix (see page 12 for recipe)
- 1 1/2 teaspoons chicken bouillon powder
- 3 tablespoons Earth Balance
- 1/4 cup all purpose flour
- 1 2/3 cups Simple Truth unsweetened almond milk

DIRECTIONS
1. In a saucepan, heat oil on medium heat.
2. Cook mushrooms and chicken bouillon 5 to 6 minutes.
3. Remove mushrooms along with the juice from pan, and set aside.
4. In the same saucepan, melt Earth Balance on medium high heat.
5. Add Bobbie's house mix and flour to saucepan. Combine well with a spoon.
6. Add almond milk and cook 2 to 3 minutes or until thick. Stir occasionally.
7. Add mushrooms and cook 2 minutes, occasionally stirring.
8. Use sauce in one of my recipes or serve over rice.

TIP
Store in refrigerator in a glass jar or plastic airtight container with a lid. Discard after 1 week.

WAKE N' BAKE

Breakfast and Brunch Dishes

SHRIMP &
GRITS

MAKES 4 SERVINGS

There are many ways to make Shrimp & Grits but my secret is okra. A small amount of okra gives this dish that southern taste you need to fully enjoy Shrimp & Grits.

FOR THE SHRIMP

- 1 pound raw shrimp, peeled and deveined
- 3 tablespoons Earth Balance
- 1/2 tablespoon Cajun seasoning
- 1/2 teaspoon minced garlic
- 1/4 teaspoon chicken bouillon powder
- 1 cup Kroger's frozen bell pepper and onion mix
- 2 tablespoons finely diced okra
- 1 tablespoon all purpose flour
- 1/2 cup Simple Truth unsweetened almond milk

DIRECTIONS

1. In a nonstick skillet, melt Earth Balance on medium heat.
2. Add bell pepper and onion mix, Cajun seasoning, garlic powder, chicken bouillon, and okra. Cook 4 to 5 minutes, occasionally stirring with a spatula.
3. Add shrimp and cook 4 to 5 minutes, occasionally stirring.
4. Stir in flour until well combined.
5. Add almond milk and cook 1 to 2 minutes, occasionally stirring.
6. Remove from heat and serve on top of grits.

FOR THE GRITS

- 3 cups Simple Truth unsweetened almond milk
- 2 tablespoons Earth Balance
- 1/2 cup quick grits
- 2 green onions, chopped
- 1/4 cup Follow Your Heart parmesan style shredded cheese

DIRECTIONS

1. In a saucepan, heat almond milk and Earth Balance on high and bring to boil.
2. Add grits and lower heat to medium. Cook 4 to 5 minutes or until soft. Stir occasionally with a spatula.
3. Add cheese and green onions.
4. Place grits on plate, add shrimp on top, and serve immediately.

ANGEL EGGS
WITH FRIED OYSTERS

MAKES 24 SERVINGS

Ain't no devils around here! Adding fried oysters to these Angel Eggs takes your brunch to another level.

FOR THE EGGS
- 12 eggs
- 1/4 cup plus 3 tablespoons mayonnaise
- 1 teaspoon stone ground mustard
- 2 teaspoons granulated sugar
- 1/4 teaspoon salt
- 1/4 teaspoon garlic powder
- 1/4 teaspoon onion powder
- 1/2 teaspoon Hot & Sweet jalapeños

DIRECTIONS
1. In a medium pot, add eggs and cover with water. Heat on high until water begins to boil. Let it cook for 1 minute, then cover and turn off heat. Leave covered for 15 minutes, then rinse under cold water for 1 minute.
2. Crack egg shells and carefully peel under cool running water. Gently dry with paper towels. Slice the eggs in half lengthwise, and place the whites on a serving platter and the yolks in a mixing bowl.
3. Mash the yolks into a fine crumble using a fork.
4. Add remaining ingredients and mix well with a hand mixer.
5. Scoop mixture into a freezer bag and push to one corner of the bag. Cut the tip of the corner and squeeze mixture into the egg whites.
6. Add fried oysters on top.

FOR THE OYSTERS
- 1 jar of oysters
- 1/4 cup seasoned flour (see page 13 for recipe)
- Oil for frying

DIRECTIONS
1. Heat cast iron skillet filled half of the way with oil to medium high. To test temperature, place end of a wooden spoon standing up to the bottom of the skillet. If it bubbles right away, it is ready.
2. Cut large oysters in small pieces and pat dry. Place oysters in quart size freezer bag and add seasoned flour. Close bag and shake until well coated.
3. Place pieces in heated oil. Cook 1 minute on each side. Remove and place oysters on a paper towel to drain. Place on top of eggs and serve.

TIP

If some of your eggs crack while boiling, or get damaged while removing the shell, still use the yolk to make the stuffing for the egg whites. You can chop up the damaged egg whites and add them to a salad.

FRENCH TOAST
WITH CREAM "CHEESE" TOPPING

MAKES 4 SERVINGS

One thing I miss since giving up dairy is Cinnabon. I didn't eat them often but the option was always there. This french toast is the next best thing.

- 3 large eggs
- 1/2 cup Simple Truth unsweetened almond milk
- 2 tablespoons Earth Balance, melted, plus more for skillet or griddle
- 1/2 teaspoon ground cinnamon
- 2 tablespoons granulated sugar
- 2 tablespoons tightly packed brown sugar
- 1/4 teaspoon nutmeg
- 1/2 teaspoon pure vanilla bean paste
- 8 slices dairy-free bread of your choice

DIRECTIONS
1. In a mixing bowl, using a whisk, combine the first 8 ingredients together.
2. Dip bread in mixture on both sides and place on a nonstick skillet or griddle coated with PAM or Earth Balance. Cook about 1 1/2 minutes on medium-high heat on each side, or until golden brown.
3. Spread with topping and serve.

CREAM "CHEESE" TOPPING
- 2 tablespoons tightly packed brown sugar
- 1/2 cup Trader Joe's vegan cream cheese
- 1 teaspoon pure vanilla bean paste
- 1 tablespoon melted Earth Balance

DIRECTIONS
1. In a mixing bowl, with a spatula, combine all ingredients together.

OPTION
You may substitute the pure vanilla bean paste for vanilla extract.

"CHEESY" SCRAMBLED
EGGS

MAKES 4 SERVINGS

The key to making perfectly scrambled eggs is cooking them slow in a nonstick skillet.

- 8 eggs
- 1/4 cup Simple Truth unsweetened almond milk
- 3 slices Follow Your Heart provolone cheese, finely chopped
- 1/4 teaspoon Ac'cent flavor enhancer
- 1/4 teaspoon salt
- 1/4 teaspoon black pepper
- 2 tablespoons Earth Balance
- 2 green onions, finely sliced for garnish

DIRECTIONS
1. In a mixing bowl, using a whisk, combine the first 6 ingredients.
2. In a nonstick skillet, melt Earth Balance on medium heat.
3. Add eggs and cook 2 to 3 minutes. Stir occasionally with a spatula.
4. Remove from heat and serve.

SPICY
POTATOES

MAKES 4 SERVINGS

No matter what time of day it is, these spicy potatoes are always a good choice.

- 4 cups peeled and chopped Russet potatoes (1/2 inch pieces)
- 1 teaspoon minced garlic
- 1 cup Kroger's frozen bell peppers and onion mix
- 1 teaspoon salt
- 1/4 teaspoon Ac'cent flavor enhancer
- 1/4 teaspoon black pepper

- 1/2 teaspoon sweet or plain paprika
- 1 garlic clove, crushed
- 1 teaspoon dried parsley
- 1/2 teaspoon finely chopped habanero pepper
- 1 tablespoon olive oil
- 2 tablespoons melted Earth Balance

DIRECTIONS
1. Preheat oven to 400 degrees F.
2. In a large bowl, with a spoon, combine all ingredients together, and place in a 9x9-inch baking pan.
3. Bake 40 to 50 minutes or until tender.
4. Remove from oven and serve.

THE MORNING AFTER
SANDWICH

MAKES 4 SERVINGS

Every so often I take medicated edibles for pain. Clearly I didn't know how strong these were because I was sitting on the couch and out of nowhere I felt the effects of the cannabis. Shortly after that I was hungry, of course, but there was nothing cooked. I whipped up this sandwich and I felt like it was the best breakfast sandwich I had ever tasted. The next morning I made it again to make sure I didn't love it just because I was high. #itwasstillbomb. I love the combination of sweet and savory flavors in breakfast dishes.

- 8 slices turkey bacon
- PAM cooking spray
- 4 eggs
- 1/4 teaspoon salt
- 1/4 teaspoon Ac'cent flavor enhancer
- 1/4 teaspoon black pepper
- 4 slices Follow Your Heart provolone style slices
- 1/2 cup fresh spinach
- 8 slices Artesano wheat bread
- 1/4 cup strawberry jelly or jam

DIRECTIONS

1. In a large skillet, on medium-high heat, spray with PAM and cook turkey bacon until crisp. Remove turkey bacon and set aside.
2. Clean skillet, then spray with PAM again and crack eggs. Do this gently so the yolk stays in tact. Evenly distribute salt, pepper, and Ac'cent flavor enhancer to all 4 eggs. Cook 2 minutes and flip. Add a slice of provolone on top of each egg and cover with a lid until melted.
3. Meanwhile, arrange bread on clean, smooth surface. Spread 1 tablespoon of jelly or jam on each of the four slices. Place cooked turkey bacon on top. Add spinach and fried egg with "cheese." Place a slice of bread on top of each.
4. Wipe out skillet, spray with PAM and place 4 sandwiches on it. Spray the top of bread with more PAM. Flip after 1 to 2 minutes or until golden brown.
5. Serve with your favorite fruit, or potatoes.

WE BEEFIN? NAH, YOU CHICKEN

Meat and Poultry Dishes

CAJUN CHICKEN
& RICE BAKE

MAKES 4 SERVINGS

I love making this dish. It's a hit with adults and children. I can honestly eat Cream of Mushroom Sauce everyday.

FOR THE CHICKEN
- 4 chicken thighs
- 1 tablespoon Canola oil
- 1/2 tablespoon Cajun seasoning
- 1/2 teaspoon onion powder

FOR THE RICE
- 1 cup uncooked rice
- 1 1/2 cups water
- 1/2 teaspoon Cajun seasoning
- 1 teaspoon dried thyme
- 1/2 teaspoon chicken bouillon powder
- 1 cup cream of mushroom sauce (see page 21 for recipe)

DIRECTIONS
1. Preheat oven to 350 degrees F.
2. In a cast iron skillet, heat oil on high.
3. Evenly coat Cajun seasoning and onion powder over 4 chicken thighs. Add thighs to cast iron skillet and sear on each side for 2 minutes.
4. Meanwhile, in a medium bowl, combine all ingredients for the rice and pour in a 9x13-inch baking dish.
5. Add chicken thighs on top, skin side up, and bake 1 hour and 15 minutes.
6. Remove from oven and serve.

SMOTHERED
SHORT RIBS

MAKES 4 SERVINGS

Short ribs have to be one of my favorite things to eat. I've had them prepared many ways but smothered has to be the best route for me.

- 2 pounds short ribs, fat trimmed
- 2 tablespoons Canola oil
- 1/4 cup plus 2 tablespoons seasoned flour (see page 13 for recipe)
- 1 (12 ounce) bag frozen black eyed peas
- 1 (12 ounce) bag Kroger's frozen bell pepper and onion mix
- 2 cups beef broth
- 2 teaspoons chicken bouillon powder
- 2 teaspoons Bobbie's house mix (see page 12 for recipe)
- Cooked rice for serving

DIRECTIONS
1. In a cast iron skillet, heat 1 tablespoon oil on high.
2. In a large freezer bag, add short ribs with 1/4 cup seasoned flour. Close bag and shake vigorously.
3. Add coated short ribs to the cast iron skillet. Cook about 1 minute on each side.
4. Place the short ribs, black eyed peas, bell peppers and onions, chicken bouillon and broth in crock pot. Cook on high 4 to 5 hours.
5. In a small saucepan, heat 1 tablespoon oil on high heat. Add 2 tablespoons seasoned flour and stir with a spatula. Cook 5 minutes stirring occasionally.
6. Add 1 cup of liquid from crockpot to the saucepan. Stir until the lumps are removed. Add back to the crockpot and stir.
7. Cook 30 minutes.
8. Serve over rice.

OPTION
You can purchase the short ribs bone in or boneless.

TURKEY HAM
& BROCCOLI CASSEROLE

MAKES 6 SERVINGS

My mother has been making this dish for us since I was a little girl. I loved it then and love it more now since I can still enjoy it while being dairy free.

- 5 3/4 cups water
- 1 cup uncooked rice
- 1 teaspoon salt
- 1/4 cup Earth Balance plus 1 tablespoon melted
- 1/4 cup all purpose flour
- 3/4 cup finely chopped onion
- 1 3/4 cups Simple Truth unsweetened almond milk
- 2 cups chopped turkey ham (I use Jenni-O)
- 1/4 teaspoon black pepper
- 2 cups broccoli
- 3 slices dairy-free bread, cubed

DIRECTIONS

FOR THE RICE
1. In a saucepan, bring 1 3/4 cups water to a boil on high heat.
2. Add 1/2 teaspoon salt and rice. Stir once to separate the rice. Cover with lid and reduce heat to low. Simmer 20 minutes.
3. Remove from fire to another eye (burner) on the stove.

FOR THE CREAM SAUCE
1. In a small pot, melt 1/4 cup Earth Balance on medium-high heat.
2. Add flour, onions, and stir with spoon until well combined.
3. Pour in almond milk a little at a time and constantly stir. Cook 2 to 3 minutes.
4. Add turkey ham, 1/2 teaspoon salt, and pepper. Stir, reduce heat to medium, and cook 5 minutes. Stir occasionally.
5. Turn off heat and keep on the eye of the stove.

FOR THE BROCCOLI
1. In a saucepan, bring 1 quart of water to a boil on high heat. Add broccoli and cook 1 minute. Drain, place in a bowl, and set aside.

TO ASSEMBLE
1. Preheat oven to 350 degrees F.
2. In a 8x8-inch baking dish, in order, add rice, broccoli, and cream sauce. Top with bread and pour 1 tablespoon melted Earth Balance evenly on top.
3. Bake 30 minutes or until bread is golden brown.
4. Remove from oven and serve.

SHORT RIB
MELT

MAKES 4 SERVINGS

This is my cousin Karmelia's favorite sandwich. She wants it every time she comes over. The flavor combination in this dish are amazing so I understand what all the fuss is about.

FOR THE SHORT RIBS

- 2 pounds short ribs, bone in or out
- 1 tablespoon Bobbie's house mix (see page 12 for recipe)
- 2 cups Kroger's frozen bell pepper and onion mix
- 1 cup beef broth
- 1 teaspoon minced garlic
- 2 tablespoons Worcestershire sauce
- 1/2 teaspoon crushed red peppers
- 1 tablespoon granulated sugar

DIRECTIONS

1. In a large bowl, combine Bobbie's house mix and short ribs.
2. In a cast iron skillet, heat up oil on high.
3. Add the short ribs and cook 1 minute on each side.
4. Remove short ribs and add to crock pot.
5. Add remaining ingredients and cook 4 to 5 hours or until tender.
6. Remove from crockpot and cut as much fat off as possible and set aside in a bowl.

FOR THE SANDWICH

- 1 tomato, thinly sliced (8 slices needed)
- Fresh spinach leaves
- 4 slices Follow Your Heart provolone style slices
- 8 Artesano bread slices
- PAM cooking spray
- Chimichurri sauce (see page 17 for recipe)

DIRECTIONS

1. Place rack in oven on second from the top slot. Preheat oven to broil.
2. Line a baking sheet with foil. Pair two tomato slices close together slightly overlapping on baking sheet. Add a few spinach leaves on top. Place one slice of provolone on each pair. Broil 1 to 2 minutes. Remove from oven.
3. Lay bread slices on a smooth surface and spread heaping amount of Chimichurri sauce on 4 of them.
4. Add a pair of tomatoes topped with provolone and generous amount of short ribs on one slice of bread. Place other slice of bread on top.
5. In a large skillet, on medium-high heat, spray PAM cooking spray. Working in batches, place sandwich in skillet and spray the top with PAM. Cook 1 to 2 minutes per side or until golden brown.

CHICKEN
BALLS

MAKES 24 BALLS

My cousin Carly makes chicken balls that our family loves because it's a classic combination of chicken, cheese, and buffalo sauce. I was inspired to change up the flavor profile and do something different.

- 2 cups finely chopped rotisserie chicken
- 1/2 cup finely chopped fire roasted red bell peppers
- 1/2 cup Daiya mozzarella style shreds, finely diced
- 1 1/2 tablespoons parsley
- 2 eggs
- 1/2 teaspoon salt
- 1/4 teaspoon black pepper
- 1 teaspoon onion powder
- 1/2 teaspoon garlic powder
- 1 tablespoon tomato paste
- 1/2 cup bread crumbs
- Oil for frying

DIRECTIONS
1. In a mixing bowl, with a spatula, combine first 10 ingredients.
2. Using a tablespoon measurement, make balls and place on parchment paper lined baking sheet. Refrigerate 1 hour.
3. Heat a short and wide pot filled half of the way with oil to medium-high. To test temperature, place end of wooden spoon standing up to the bottom of the skillet. If it bubbles right away, it is ready.
4. In a small bowl, add bread crumbs and roll the balls in bowl until fully coated.
5. Add balls to pot 6 to 8 at a time. Cook 1 1/2 minutes or until golden brown.
6. Remove from heat and place on a paper towel to drain.
7. Serve with dipping sauce.

FOR THE DIPPING SAUCE
- 2 tablespoons Follow Your Heart vegan ranch dressing
- 1 teaspoon tomato paste
- 1/2 teaspoon honey
- Pinch cayenne pepper

DIRECTIONS
1. In a small bowl, with a spatula, combine all ingredients.

TIP
To freeze, place balls on a parchment paper lined baking sheet and put in the freezer for 1 hour or until balls are hard. Remove from baking sheet and place in freezer bag. To cook, unthaw, dip in bread crumbs and follow frying directions.

CURRY CHICKEN
POT PIE

MAKES 6 SERVINGS

If a Jamaican patty and a pot pie had a baby this is what it would be. Make this for your friends and watch the compliments roll in.

FOR THE CHICKEN
- 1 pound boneless, skinless chicken breast tenders
- 2 tablespoons olive oil
- 2 tablespoons curry powder
- 2 teaspoons salt

DIRECTIONS
1. Preheat oven to 350 degrees F.
2. In a mixing bowl, with clean hands, combine all ingredients.
3. Place on baking sheet and bake 15 minutes.
4. Remove from oven and set aside in a clean bowl.

FOR THE POTATOES
- 2 cups peeled and diced Russet potatoes, 1/2 inch pieces
- 5 cups water
- 1 teaspoon salt

DIRECTIONS
1. In a medium sized pot, add all ingredients and boil 10 minutes.
2. Drain and place in bowl with cooked chicken.

FOR THE FILLING
- 2 tablespoons olive oil
- 1/2 cup chopped red bell pepper
- 1/2 cup chopped sweet onion
- 1/2 cup chopped celery
- 1 1/2 teaspoons salt
- 1/4 teaspoon black pepper
- 1/4 teaspoon chicken bouillon powder
- 2 teaspoons granulated sugar
- 1 (14.5 ounce) can coconut cream
- 2 prepared pie crust

DIRECTIONS
1. Preheat oven to 350 degrees F. Place one of the pie crusts in an 9 x 9-inch baking dish and bake 15 minutes. Remove from oven.
2. Meanwhile, in a medium sized pot, add first 7 ingredients and cook on medium heat for 15 minutes. Stir occasionally with a spatula.
3. Add sugar and coconut cream. Cook 2 to 3 minutes then add cooked chicken and cooked potatoes. Stir with spatula until well combined.
4. Pour mixture in baking dish and place pie crust on top. Pinch the edges to seal it. Cut 3 slits in the top to release steam.
5. Bake 25 to 30 minutes, or until golden brown.
6. Remove from oven and serve.

We Beefin? Nah, You Chicken   49

BBQ
SPAGHETTI

MAKES 8 SERVINGS

When I say BBQ spaghetti, no one can wrap their head around the combination of pasta noodles, BBQ sauce, and cheese. Do not be afraid, this combination is something you have to try.

- 1 pound ground beef
- 2 chicken andouille sausage links, chopped
- 1 green bell pepper, finely chopped
- 1/2 cup finely chopped onions
- 1 teaspoon onion powder
- 2 cups Sweet Baby Ray's BBQ sauce
- 1 garlic clove, crushed
- 3 slices Follow Your Heart provolone style slices, finely chopped
- 1 (16 ounce) bag or box of spaghetti noodles
  (use cooking instructions based on your liking).
- 1 green onion, chopped

DIRECTIONS
1. In a medium pot, on medium-high heat, add the first 5 ingredients.
2. Cook 5 to 6 minutes or until ground beef is no longer pink.
3. Add BBQ sauce, garlic, and provolone.
4. Add cooked noodles and stir in green onions.

OPTION
If you don't eat beef you can always use 1 pound ground turkey. Follow the directions but 1 to 2 extra minutes may be needed to cook the ground turkey all the way through.

BEEF CHORIZO
BURGER & FRIES

MAKES 6 SERVINGS

I came up with this burger by accident. I wanted to make burgers one night but only had a little bit of ground meat. I added beef chorizo and this star was born!

FOR THE BURGER

- 1 pound ground beef
- 1 pound beef chorizo
- 1/2 cup grated onions
- 1/2 teaspoon salt
- 1/4 teaspoon black pepper
- 1 teaspoon garlic powder
- 1 teaspoon onion powder
- 2 teaspoons dried parsley
- 6 slices turkey bacon, cooked
- 6 Follow Your Heart provolone style slices
- Lettuce
- Tomato slices
- Artesano burger buns, toasted
- Special sauce (see page 19 for recipe)

DIRECTIONS

1. In a mixing bowl, using your hands, combine the first 8 ingredients together. Using a 1/2 cup measuring cup make a ball. Flatten it to make a 4 inch patty.
2. Heat up a large cast iron skillet to medium-high heat and add patties. Cook 2 minutes on each side. Place pan in oven and cook 10 minutes. Place one slice of turkey bacon then provolone on each patty and cook about 2 minutes. Remove from oven and place patties on plate.
3. On a flat surface place bottom bun down. Add special sauce, lettuce, tomatoes, and cooked patties. Add more special sauce to the top bun and place over patties.

FOR THE FRIES

- 5 Russet potatoes, sliced
- Oil for frying
- 1 teaspoon dried parsley
- 1/2 teaspoon Cajun seasoning
- 1/4 teaspoon granulated sugar
- 1/4 cup Follow Your Heart parmesan shredded cheese

DIRECTIONS

1. Heat large and wide pot filled half of the way with oil to medium high heat. To test temperature, place end of wooden spoon standing up to the bottom of the skillet. If it bubbles right away, it is ready.
2. Add potatoes and cook 10 to 12 minutes or until golden brown. Remove from oil and place in a paper towel lined bowl.
3. Meanwhile, in a mixing bowl, with a spoon, combine remaining ingredients.
4. Remove paper towel from bowl and toss the fries in the mixture.

OPTION

Feel free to use 1 pound ground turkey with soy or chicken chorizo. Follow the directions but add a few minutes to your cooking time.

GREAT CATCH

Seafood Dishes

ASHTON'S MARVELOUS
MUSSELS

MAKES 6 SERVINGS

My friend Aisha has two amazing young boys that love to cook named Ashton and Aven. When I asked her if she wanted to add a dish to my cookbook, she asked if it could be one of the boys' recipes. I said yes but it has to be delicious. Ashton did the damn thang! I changed it slightly but kept the vibe of the dish.

- 2 pounds fresh mussels, scrubbed and cleaned
- 2 tablespoons olive oil
- 1 pound beef chorizo
- 2 green onions, thinly sliced
- 4 cloves fresh garlic, thinly sliced
- 1 teaspoon sweet or plain paprika
- 1 (14.5 ounce) can fire roasted tomatoes
- 1 cup water
- 1 teaspoon chicken bouillon powder
- 3/4 teaspoon salt
- 1/4 teaspoon black pepper
- 1/4 teaspoon saffron (optional)
- 1/4 cup finely chopped fresh parsley

DIRECTIONS
1. Rinse mussels under cold running water. Remove the beard from each mussel and start scraping off any barnacles or other dirt, then add them to a bowl.
2. In a nonstick skillet, heat oil on medium-high heat.
3. Add chorizo, onions, garlic, and cook 4 to 5 minutes or until cooked through.
4. Add remaining ingredients except mussels. Cook 4 to 5 minutes, stirring occasionally.
5. Add mussels into the pan, move them around so they are all evenly distributed. Place a lid on the pan and reduce the heat to low. Cook 5 to 6 minutes.
6. Remove the lid. Check to make sure all mussels are opened. Discard unopened mussels.
7. Remove from heat and serve with your favorite non-dairy bread.

JERK SALMON
WITH COCONUT RICE

MAKES 4 SERVINGS

My bestie Tasha loves salmon. I never liked it until I realized I was always eating it overcooked. I started making it at home, cooking it to my liking, and fell in love.

FOR THE SALMON

- 4 salmon pieces
- 1 teaspoon ground cinnamon
- 1 teaspoon all-spice
- 1 teaspoon dried thyme
- 1 tablespoon brown sugar
- 2 garlic cloves, crushed
- 1 tablespoon grated onion
- 1 tablespoon green onions
- 1 tablespoon vinegar
- 2 tablespoons olive oil
- 1 tablespoon lime juice
- 3/4 teaspoon salt
- 1/4 teaspoon black pepper

DIRECTIONS
1. In a mixing bowl, with a spatula, combine all ingredients excluding the salmon.
2. Place salmon in a large freezer bag, add mixture and close.
3. Marinate 2 to 8 hours.

COOKING THE SALMON
1. Preheat oven to 350 degrees F.
2. Place salmon on a baking sheet lined with foil.
3. Bake 18 to 20 minutes.
4. Remove from oven and serve with rice.

FOR THE COCONUT RICE

- 1 cup uncooked rice
- 1/4 teaspoon salt
- 1 3/4 cups water
- 1/2 cup coconut cream from a can
- 2 tablespoons granulated sugar

DIRECTIONS
1. In a saucepan, bring water, rice, and salt to a boil on high heat.
2. Reduce heat to low, cover with a lid, and cook 20 minutes.
3. Turn off the fire and stir in coconut cream and sugar. Let it sit 5 minutes.
4. Remove from heat and serve.

OPTION
This marinade is great on other seafood. Shrimp is a delicious substitute for the salmon. Use 1 pound shrimp, peeled and deveined. Follow the directions but cook the shrimp 6 to 8 minutes or until pink and cooked through.

OYSTER PO' BOY
WITH CHIPOTLE MAYO

MAKES 4 PO' BOYS

If you're an oyster lover like me you will love this sandwich. I have never been to New Orleans (I know shame on me) but I imagine I'd find plenty of these Po' Boys out there.

- 2 jars of oysters, drained
- 1/2 cup seasoned flour (see page 13 for recipe)
- Oil for frying
- 4 french rolls
- 1 large tomato, sliced
- Lettuce, shredded
- Red onions, sliced

DIRECTIONS
1. Heat cast iron skillet filled half of the way with oil to medium-high heat. To test temperature, place end of wooden spoon standing up to the bottom of the skillet. If it bubbles right away, it is ready.
2. Place oysters in a quart sized freezer bag and add seasoned flour. Close bag and shake until well coated. Place oysters in heated oil. Cook 1 to 2 minutes on each side. Remove oysters and place on a paper towel to drain.
3. Split the rolls; spread chipotle mayo on both sides. On the bottom of the roll, put lettuce, tomatoes, red onions, and oysters.

CHIPOTLE MAYO
- 1/4 cup Best Foods mayo
- 1 tablespoon liquid from can of Las Palmas chipotle peppers in adobo sauce
- 1/2 teaspoon honey
- 1 teaspoon fresh lemon juice
- 1 teaspoon dried parsley

DIRECTIONS
1. In a mixing bowl, with a spatula, combine all ingredients together.

TIP
Fried foods are best when eaten fresh. You can always fry just enough for a single serving and fry the rest the next day, just add less of the seasoned flour so you don't waste it.

SHRIMP & CRAB
PASTA SALAD

MAKES 8 SERVINGS

My friend Alana loves this dish. What's not to love about seafood? This sweet and savory pasta salad is the perfect addition to your dinner party.

FOR THE NOODLES

- 3 quarts water
- 1 tablespoon salt
- 2 cups elbow noodles

DIRECTIONS
1. In a medium pot, on high heat, bring water and salt to a boil.
2. Add noodles, stir 10 to 12 seconds with a spoon, and cook 7 to 8 minutes.
3. Drain, rinse with cold water, place in a bowl, and let cool for 20 minutes.

FOR THE SHRIMP

- 1 pound raw shrimp, peeled and deveined
- 1/2 teaspoon Cajun seasoning
- 1 tablespoon olive oil

DIRECTIONS
1. In a skillet, heat oil on medium-high heat.
2. Add shrimp and Cajun seasoning. Cook 2 to 3 minutes on each side.
3. Remove from heat, place in a bowl, and set aside.

FOR THE MIXTURE

- 1 (8 ounce) can lump crab meat
- 1/4 cup finely chopped green onions
- 1/2 cup finely chopped celery
- 3 tablespoons sweet pickled relish
- 1/4 teaspoon Ac'cent flavor enhancer
- 1/4 teaspoon black pepper
- 1/4 teaspoon Cajun seasoning
- 1/2 teaspoon garlic powder
- 1 1/2 cups Best Foods mayo

DIRECTIONS
1. In a large bowl, combine all ingredients with a spoon.
2. Add cooked shrimp and cooked noodles. Stir until well combined.
3. Refrigerate 4 hours.

GUMBO
LIKE UNCLE ROBBY'S

MAKES 6 SERVINGS

Growing up, my uncle Robby was the gumbo maker in the family. He was a great cook so I watched him every chance I got, and after he had a stroke I started to make gumbo for the family. It has become our tradition to have it at Christmas. He is not fully recovered but he always says "Gumbo's good Bobbie," and it's all thanks to him.

- 6 cups water
- Shrimp shells
- 1 (12 ounce) bag Kroger's cut okra
- 3 tablespoons Canola oil
- 1/3 cup seasoned flour (see page 13 for recipe)
- 2 andouille chicken sausage links, finely chopped
- 1 cup chopped celery
- 1 cup chopped green bell pepper
- 1 cup chopped onion
- 1 (8 ounce) bottle clam juice

- 1 (14.5 ounce) can diced tomatoes with roasted garlic
- 1 garlic clove, crushed
- 1 tablespoon chicken bouillon powder
- 1 teaspoon Cajun seasoning
- 3 bay leaves
- 1/2 pound crab legs
- 1 (8ounce) can lump crab
- 1/4 teaspoon cayenne pepper
- 1 tablespoon dried parsley
- 2 chicken thighs, boneless and skinless
- 1 pound raw shrimp, peeled and deveined

DIRECTIONS
1. In a medium pot, bring water, shrimp shells and okra to a boil on high heat. Boil 5 minutes then remove from heat. Drain the liquid into a bowl.
2. Meanwhile, in a large pot, heat oil on medium-high.
3. Add seasoned flour and cook 9 to 10 minutes. Stir constantly using a spatula.
4. Add chicken sausage, celery, bell peppers and onions. Reduce heat to medium and cook 4 to 5 minutes.
5. Add 4 cups shrimp stock and clam juice. Stir with a whisk until well combined.
6. Add tomatoes, garlic, chicken bouillon, Cajun seasoning, bay leaves, crab legs, lump crab, and cayenne pepper. Stir with a large spoon.
7. Cover with a lid. Cook 1 hour.
8. Add chicken thighs. Cook 45 minutes to 1 hour.
9. Add shrimp and dried parsley. Cook 15 minutes.
10. Remove from heat and serve over rice.

TUNA
CASSEROLE

MAKES 6 SERVINGS

This is another one of my childhood favorites. It almost didn't make the cookbook with all of the the recipes I had to choose from, but my taste testers insisted that it be in here.

FOR THE NOODLES

- 2 1/2 quarts water
- 2 teaspoons salt
- 1 1/2 cups elbow noodles

DIRECTIONS
1. In a small pot, boil water on high heat.
2. Add salt and noodles, stir 5 seconds with a spoon, and cook 6 to 7 minutes. Drain, rinse with cold water, place in a bowl, and set aside.

FOR THE TUNA SAUCE

- 1 (7 ounce) can tuna
- 1 (8 ounce) container Trader Joe's vegan cream cheese
- 1 (2 ounce) jar pimentos
- 1/2 cup grated onions
- 1 cup cream of mushroom sauce (see page 21 for recipe)
- 3/4 teaspoon salt
- 1/4 teaspoon black pepper
- 3 slices Artesano bread, chopped in 1/2 inch pieces
- 2 tablespoons melted Earth Balance

DIRECTIONS
1. Preheat oven to 350 degrees F.
2. In a medium pot, add the first 7 ingredients. Cook on medium-high heat for 5 minutes.
3. Add cooked noodles and stir until well combined.
4. Pour in 9x9-inch baking dish.
5. Sprinkle bread on top and pour Earth Balance evenly over it.
6. Bake 30 minutes or until bread is golden brown.
7. Remove from oven and serve.

CLAM
CHOWDER

MAKES 4 SERVINGS

The plan was to make my mom's famous salmon chowder but there is something about clams that sits well in my spirit so clam chowder it is!

- 2 cups peeled and chopped Russet potatoes, cut in 1/2 inch pieces.
- 1 quart water
- 3/4 cup chopped onions
- 1 cup chopped celery
- 1/4 cup Earth Balance
- 1/4 cup all purpose flour
- 1 1/2 cups Simple Truth unsweetened almond milk
- 1 teaspoon salt
- 1/4 teaspoon black pepper
- 1 garlic clove, crushed
- 1/2 teaspoon onion powder
- 1/2 teaspoon chicken bouillon powder
- 2 (6.5 ounce) cans minced clams, juice included

DIRECTIONS

1. In a medium saucepan, bring water, potatoes, onions, celery, and 1/2 teaspoon salt to a boil on high heat. Cook 10 minutes. Drain, place in a bowl, and set aside.
2. Meanwhile, in a medium pot, heat Earth Balance on medium-high heat.
3. Add flour and stir with a spatula until combined.
4. Add almond milk, salt, pepper, garlic, onion powder, and chicken bouillon, and stir until thick.
5. Add cooked potatoes and cans of minced clams. Cook 1 to 2 minutes.
6. Remove from heat and serve with corn muffins or garlic toast.

VEGAN ON THE WEEKEND

Plant-Based Dishes

MUSHROOM
& SPINACH QUESADILLA

MAKES 4 SERVINGS

Dennis is one of my best friends and a taste tester for this cookbook. He was skeptical about trying this recipe because he didn't know how the "cheese" would melt and how the dish would taste. After trying it he loved it and said it didn't make him miss eating meat at all.

- 1 tablespoon olive oil plus extra for coating the skillet
- 1 (8 ounce) pack mushrooms, thinly sliced
- 1 1/2 cups Kroger's frozen bell pepper and onion mix
- 2 teaspoons blackened spice (see page 12 for recipe)
- 1/2 teaspoon ground sweet basil
- 1 bunch fresh spinach
- Daiya mozzarella style shreds
- 4 flour tortillas

DIRECTIONS
1. In a large skillet, heat 1 tablespoon oil on medium-high heat.
2. Add mushrooms, bell peppers and onions, blackened spice, and sweet basil. Cook 8 to 9 minutes. Stir occasionally with a spatula.
3. Turn off the fire and add spinach. Stir 4 to 5 times to not wilt the spinach completely. Remove from skillet and place in a bowl.
4. Place tortillas on a large cutting board. Add a handful of mozzarella and two spoonfuls of mushroom and spinach to one side of the tortilla. Fold the tortilla over the mixture and press down firmly. Repeat this with all 4 tortillas.
5. Clean the same skillet, and heat a small amount of oil on medium high. Place folded tortillas in your skillet and cook 1 to 2 minutes on each side or until golden brown.
6. Remove from heat and serve with dipping sauce.

DIPPING SAUCE

- 1/2 cup Tofutti's Better Than Sour Cream
- 1 teaspoon McCormick's Chimichurri seasoning
- 1 teaspoon honey
- 1/4 teaspoon salt
- 1/4 crushed red peppers

DIRECTIONS

1. In a small mixing bowl, with a spoon, combine all ingredients together.

CURRIED
CAULIFLOWER RICE

MAKES 4 SERVINGS

Not a cauliflower fan? You will love this dish and won't miss the rice at all.

- 3 tablespoons Canola oil
- 1 (12 ounce) bag cauliflower rice
- 1 cup Kroger's frozen bell pepper and onion mix
- 1 tablespoon curry powder
- 3/4 teaspoon salt
- 1 garlic clove, crushed
- 1/2 teaspoon ginger paste
- 1 1/2 tablespoons granulated sugar
- 2 cups fresh spinach

DIRECTIONS
1. In a large nonstick skillet, heat oil on medium-high heat.
2. Add cauliflower rice, bell pepper and onion, curry powder, and salt. Cook 12 to 13 minutes, stirring occasionally with a spatula.
3. Add garlic, ginger, and sugar. Cook 2 to 3 minutes.
4. Add spinach and stir until spinach is wilted and well combined.
5. Remove from heat and serve.

SCALLOPED
POTATOES

MAKES 6 SERVINGS

Creamy and delicious. Is there anything more to say?

- 3 tablespoons Earth Balance
- 3 tablespoons all purpose flour
- 1 1/2 cups Simple Truth unsweetened almond milk
- 1 teaspoon minced garlic
- 1/2 teaspoon onion powder
- 1 teaspoon salt
- Black pepper to taste
- 1/2 cup Follow Your Heart parmesan style shredded cheese
- 3 or 4 Russet potatoes, peeled and thinly sliced
- 2/3 cup grated sweet onion

DIRECTIONS

1. Preheat oven to 400 degrees F.
2. Place sliced potatoes in a bowl of water and set aside.
3. In a small pot, heat Earth Balance on medium-heat.
4. Add flour and stir with a spatula until well combined.
5. Add almond milk and stir 1 minute.
6. Add remaining ingredients and stir until well combined. Turn off the heat.
7. Drain potatoes and stir them into the pot with cream sauce.
8. Pour mixture into a 9x9-inch baking dish and cover with foil.
9. Bake 30 minutes. Remove foil and bake 25 minutes.
10. Remove from oven and serve.

SWEET
& SPICY CABBAGE

MAKES 6 SERVINGS

I love pretty much all vegetables. To keep from getting tired of them, I switch up the ingredients. The sweet n' spicy jalapeños gives me the subtle change that I need in my life.

- 3 tablespoons Canola oil
- 1 (12 ounce) bag Kroger's frozen bell pepper and onion mix
- 6 cups chopped green cabbage
- 1 teaspoon Bobbie's house mix (see page 12 for recipe)
- 1/2 teaspoon Better Than Bouillon roasted garlic base
- 1 tablespoon chopped Hot & Sweet jalapeños
- 1 tablespoon granulated sugar
- 1 teaspoon salt

DIRECTIONS
1. In a medium pot, heat oil on medium-high.
2. Add bell pepper and onion. Cook 5 to 6 minutes, occasionally stirring with a spatula.
3. Add remaining ingredients and cook 8 to 10 minutes or until cabbage is to your liking.
4. Remove from heat and serve.

BELLE'S BALSAMIC
TOMATOES

MAKES 9 TO 12 TOMATOES

Belle is one of my best friends. She has two beautiful boys and she is always cooking up things that they are not old enough to appreciate. When we talk food—which is everyday—I ask her why she doesn't make certain things for them. Her response is always "Girl you know they ain't gone eat that!" Being a picky eater will have you missing out. Don't let this blessin' pass you by.

- 2 tablespoons balsamic vinegar
- 1 tablespoon Italian seasoning
- 1/4 teaspoon salt
- 3 tomatoes
- Handful of fresh spinach
- Daiya mozzarella style shreds, finely chopped

DIRECTIONS

1. In a mixing bowl, using a whisk, combine balsamic vinegar, Italian seasoning, and salt together.
2. On a cutting board, place the tomato on its side and cut a thin slice off the top where it is connected to the vine and the bottom. These two pieces will not be used so you can discard or cut up and use later.
3. Slice one tomato into 3 to 4 slices. Continue this process with remaining tomatoes.
4. Add tomatoes to bowl of balsamic vinegar. Turn the tomatoes over a couple of times in the mixture so they are well coated.
5. Place tomatoes and liquid in a large freezer bag. Seal tightly and place the bag on a dinner plate. Spread the tomatoes inside the bag so they are as flat as possible. Place both bag and plate in the refrigerator for at least 4 hours.
6. Preheat oven to 400 degrees F.
7. On a baking sheet lined with foil, place tomatoes down, add 1 to 2 leaves of spinach, and sprinkle a little mozzarella on top.
8. Bake 15 minutes. Remove from oven and serve.

SOY CHORIZO
& POTATO SOUP

MAKES 4 TO 6 SERVINGS

I made this recipe by chance. While creating the last few recipes for my cookbook I decided to use everything in my cupboard and pantry before buying more ingredients for dishes, and that was the best decision ever. This soup is so tasty.

- 2 cups Russet potatoes, peeled and cut in 1/2 inch cubes
- 6 1/2 cups water
- 1/4 cup olive oil
- 1 cup finely chopped celery
- 2 cups Kroger's frozen bell pepper and onion mix
- 1 teaspoon finely chopped jalapeños
- 1 pound soy chorizo
- 1 teaspoon salt
- Black pepper to taste
- 2 teaspoons Better Than Bouillon roasted garlic base
- 1 (15.5 ounce) can Northwestern beans
-

DIRECTIONS

1. In a medium pot, boil 1 quart of water, 1/2 teaspoon salt, and potatoes for 10 minutes on high. Drain, place in a bowl, and set aside.
2. Meanwhile, in a medium sized pot, heat oil on medium-high heat. Add celery, bell peppers, onions, and jalapeños, and cook 10 minutes. Stir occasionally with a spatula.
3. Add chorizo and cook 5 minutes. Stir occasionally with a spatula.
4. Add 2 1/2 cups water, 1/2 teaspoon salt, pepper, Better Than Bouillon, beans, and cooked potatoes. Cook 10 minutes stirring occasionally.
5. Remove from heat and serve.

COCONUT SOUP
WITH SHIITAKE MUSHROOMS

MAKES 6 SERVINGS

One of my favorite restaurants in Los Angeles has a chicken coconut soup that I love. When I created this recipe my intention was to make it without meat and have it still taste amazing. Mission accomplished in my opinion.

- 3 tablespoons olive oil
- 2 cups shiitake mushrooms
- 2/3 cup grated onions
- 1 garlic clove, crushed
- 1 teaspoon ginger paste
- 2 (15 ounce) cans coconut cream
- 1/4 teaspoon Ac'cent flavor enhancer
- 1 teaspoon salt
- 1/2 teaspoon black pepper
- 1 tablespoon chopped cilantro
- 1 tablespoon chopped green onions

DIRECTIONS
1. In a medium pot, heat oil on medium-high.
2. Add mushrooms and onions. Cook 6 to 7 minutes or until tender. Stir occasionally with a spatula.
3. Add remaining ingredients and cook on medium heat for 10 minutes. Stir occasionally with a spatula.
4. Remove from heat and serve.

OH, THAT'S EXTRA

Side Dishes

CRAB & MANGO
GUACAMOLE

MAKES 6 TO 8 SERVINGS

My friend December said this was the best guacamole she had ever tasted. The lump crab meat and mango make this recipe sing!

- 2 cups avocado (about 6 small ripe ones)
- 1/4 cup finely chopped radishes
- 1/2 cup chopped tomatoes
- 2 tablespoons chopped fresh cilantro
- 1 mango, chopped
- 1 teaspoon salt
- 1/2 teaspoon garlic powder
- 1/2 teaspoon onion powder
- 3/4 teaspoon Ac'cent flavor enhancer
- 1 1/2 tablespoons finely chopped jalapeños
- 2 tablespoons chopped Hot & Sweet jalapeños
- 1 (8 ounce) can crab claw meat
- Juice from half of a lime

DIRECTIONS

1. Cut avocados in half, remove the pit, and scoop flesh into a mixing bowl.
2. Add remaining ingredients and stir with a spoon until well combined. Do not stir after each ingredient is added. This will make your guacamole runny.
3. Place in a container with a lid and refrigerate for at least 1 hour.

MUSTARD GREENS
WITH TURKEY BACON

MAKES 4 SERVINGS

This quick & easy recipe is the perfect side for dinner.

- 3 turkey bacon strips, chopped
- 2 tablespoons olive oil
- 1/4 cup grated onions
- 8 cups mustard greens, cleaned & chopped
- 1 teaspoon salt
- 1 teaspoon onion powder
- 2 garlic cloves, crushed
- Red crushed peppers to taste
- 2 teaspoons honey

DIRECTIONS
1. In a small pot, heat oil on medium-high.
2. Add turkey bacon and onions, and cook 2 to 3 minutes. Stir occasionally with a spatula.
3. Add remaining ingredients excluding honey and cook 8 to 10 minutes or until greens are tender. Stir occasionally.
4. Stir in honey until well combined.
5. Remove from heat and serve.

CORN MUFFINS
WITH HONEY SPREAD

MAKES 14 MUFFINS

I was tired of my mom making her delicious muffins right in my face so I altered her recipe to comply with my lifestyle and added a honey spread.

- 1 cup cornmeal
- 1 cup all purpose flour
- 3/4 cup granulated sugar
- 1 tablespoon baking powder
- 1/4 teaspoon salt
- 1 egg
- 1/2 cup melted Earth balance
- 1 cup Simple Truth unsweetened almond milk

DIRECTIONS
1. Preheat the oven to 400 degrees F.
2. Place cupcake liners in muffin pan.
3. In a mixing bowl, with a spatula, combine all dry ingredients together.
4. In another mixing bowl, combine all wet ingredients together.
5. Stir wet ingredients into bowl with dry ingredients.
6. Using 1/4 cup, scoop mixture and pour into each cupcake liner.
7. Bake 25 minutes.
8. Remove the corn muffins from the oven and let them cool for 10 minutes. Serve with honey spread.

HONEY SPREAD
- 1/4 cup Earth Balance
- 2 teaspoons honey
- Pinch of ground cinnamon

DIRECTIONS
1. In a small bowl, with a spoon, combine ingredients together.

MAC N' PLEASE
HOLD THE CHEESE

MAKES 4 TO 6 SERVINGS

Mac & cheese is a hard one to duplicate. I could not find a non-dairy mac & cheese that I liked anywhere. I tried to make it and kept failing. I always thought mac & cheese had to be how I ate it growing up: Orangish yellow in color and creamy. I am not a fan of any cheddar cheese alternatives, and I had given up on creating a recipe until I reminded myself that quitting ain't what we do over here. I have made what I feel is a winner winner mac for dinner.

FOR THE NOODLES
- 2 1/2 quarts water
- 1 cup elbow noodles
- 1/2 teaspoon salt

DIRECTIONS
1. In a small pot, boil water on high heat.
2. Add salt and noodles, stir 10 to 12 seconds with a spoon, and cook 7 to 8 minutes. Drain, rinse with cold water, place in a bowl, and set aside.

FOR THE SAUCE
- 1 tablespoon Earth Balance
- 1 tablespoon seasoned flour (see page 13 for recipe)
- 1/4 cup Simple Truth unsweetened almond milk
- 1 (8 ounce) container Trader Joe's vegan cream cheese
- 3/4 cup Follow Your Heart parmesan style shredded cheese
- 2 slices Follow Your Heart provolone style slices
- 1/2 cup cream of mushroom sauce (see page 21 for recipe)
- 1/2 teaspoon ground sage
- Black pepper to taste

DIRECTIONS
1. In a saucepan, heat Earth Balance on medium-high.
2. Add seasoned flour and stir with spatula until well combined.
3. Add almond milk and stir until well combined.
4. Add remaining ingredients and cook 2 to 3 minutes. Stir occasionally with a spatula.
5. Add cooked noodles into saucepan and stir until well combined.
6. Remove from heat and serve.

BAKED BEANS
WITH TURKEY BACON

MAKES 8 SERVINGS

No BBQ is complete without baked beans. Make this your contribution to the family picnic.

- 2 tablespoons Canola oil
- 8 strips turkey bacon, chopped
- 1 large green bell pepper, chopped
- 1 cup chopped sweet onions
- 1 (53 ounce) can pork and beans
- 1 cup ketchup
- 2/3 cup tightly packed brown sugar
- 1 tablespoon Worcestershire sauce
- 1 tablespoon yellow mustard
- 2 teaspoons salt
- 1/2 teaspoon black pepper

DIRECTIONS
1. Preheat oven to 350 degrees F.
2. In a medium pot, heat oil on medium-high.
3. Add turkey bacon, bell peppers and onions. Cook 5 minutes. Stir occasionally with spatula.
4. Add remaining ingredients and stir until well combined.
5. Pour beans in 9x13-inch baking dish.
6. Bake 45 minutes to 1 hour.
7. Remove from oven and serve.

COLLARD GREENS
WITH SMOKED TURKEY TAILS

MAKES 8 SERVINGS

My great grandmother taught me how to make collard greens at a very young age. I don't know how other people's grandmothers were but mine was very particular about how she cooked. She had a talent that shined through her food that was hard to replicate. I replaced the hammocks she normally used with smoked turkey tails, but I think she would be proud of these collards for sure.

- 2 (16 ounce) bags collard greens, cleaned
- 2 smoked turkey tails
- 1 (12 ounce) bag Kroger's frozen bell pepper and onion mix
- 1 teaspoon minced garlic
- 1 teaspoon salt
- 1 tablespoon chicken bouillon powder
- 1 tablespoon Worcestershire sauce
- 1/2 teaspoon finely diced habanero pepper
- 1 tablespoon vinegar
- 3 tablespoons granulated sugar
- 2 cups water

DIRECTIONS

1. In a crockpot, add all ingredients. Cook on high 4 to 5 hours or until they are to your liking. Occasionally stir with spoon.

OPTION

You can use the bags of collard, mustard, and turnip greens that come all together as well.

RED BEANS
& RICE

MAKES 4 SERVINGS

Now I love a good crockpot recipe, but sometimes I don't want to go through the process of cooking with dry beans. This recipe cuts the time but keeps the taste.

- 3 tablespoons Canola oil
- 2 cups Kroger's frozen bell pepper and onion mix
- 2 bay leaves
- 2 chicken andouille sausage links, chopped
- 2 tablespoons seasoned flour (see page 13 for recipe)
- 1 cup water
- 1 (14.5 ounce) can red beans, drained
- 1 teaspoon chicken bouillon powder
- Cooked rice for serving

DIRECTIONS
1. In a medium pot, heat oil on medium-high.
2. Add chicken andouille sausage, bell pepper and onions, and bay leaves. Cook 10 minutes or until veggies are tender. Stir occasionally with spoon.
3. Add seasoned flour and stir until well combined. Cook 5 minutes.
4. Add remaining ingredients, then reduce heat to low and cook 30 minutes. Stir occasionally with spoon.
5. Remove from heat, take out bay leaves, and serve over rice.

GIMME SOME SUGAH

Desserts and Drinks

KARM'S
COCKTAIL

MAKES 1 COCKTAIL

My cousin Karmen loves to host just like I do. It's funny how she thinks she's the only one who knows how to make a good cocktail. I have to give her credit where it is due for this one though. She made this cocktail for us and it's been "Karm can you make that cocktail" ever since. I altered the measurements but the magic that Karmen created is still there.

- 1/4 cup Effen Black Cherry Vanilla Vodka
- 2 teaspoons simple syrup
- 1 egg white
- Handful of ice
- 1/2 cup Simply Lemonade
- Fresh rosemary for garnish
- Cocktail shaker

DIRECTIONS
1. In a shaker, add all ingredients except rosemary. Shake vigorously until cocktail is frothy.
2. Pour in glass and garnish with rosemary.

OPTION
Swap the vodka for whatever liquor you prefer. Peach Ciroc in place of the Effen vodka is delicious too!

STRAWBERRY
JELL-O CAKE

MAKES 16 SERVINGS

This recipe reminds me of my childhood with an extra pinch of goodness added.

FOR THE CAKE
- 1 box strawberry cake
- 1 box strawberry Jell-O
- 4 eggs
- 3/4 cup Canola oil
- 1 cup water

DIRECTIONS
1. Preheat oven to 350 degrees F.
2. Prepare bundt pan by lightly greasing and flouring the pan.
3. In a mixing bowl, using a hand mixer, combine all ingredients together.
4. Pour into bundt cake pan and bake 35 min.
5. Let cool for 20 to 30 minutes.
6. Remove from pan by placing plate on top and flip. Place another plate on top and flip again.
7. Glaze and serve.

FOR THE GLAZE
- 1 cup powdered sugar
- 2 1/2 tablespoons water

DIRECTIONS
1. In a mixing bowl, with a spatula, combine all ingredients together.

BANANA NUT
CAKE

SERVES 16

This one is certainly a crowd pleaser for breakfast, brunch, or dessert.

FOR THE CAKE

- 3 cups all purpose flour
- 1 teaspoon salt
- 1 cup granulated sugar
- 1/2 cup tightly packed brown sugar
- 1 1/2 teaspoons ground cinnamon
- 1 tablespoon baking powder
- 1/2 teaspoon baking soda
- 1 teaspoon pure vanilla bean paste
- 1 1/2 cups Canola oil
- 1 1/2 cups Simple Truth unsweetened almond milk
- 1 banana, mashed
- 2 eggs
- 1/2 cup finely chopped walnuts

DIRECTIONS
1. Preheat oven to 350 degrees F.
2. Prepare bundt pan by lightly greasing and flouring the pan.
3. In a mixing bowl, using a spatula, combine all dry ingredients together.
4. In another mixing bowl, using a whisk, combine all wet ingredients and banana.
5. Using a hand mixer, combine wet ingredients into dry ingredients. There will be lumps from banana.
6. Stir in walnuts.
7. Pour cake batter into prepared baking pan and bake 50 minutes.
8. Remove from oven. Let cool for 20 to 30 minutes. Remove from pan by placing plate on top and flip. Place another plate on top and flip again.
9. Glaze and serve.

FOR THE GLAZE

- 1 cup powdered sugar
- 1/4 teaspoon ground cinnamon
- 1/2 teaspoon pure vanilla bean paste
- 2 1/2 tablespoons water

DIRECTIONS
1. In a small bowl, with a spatula, combine all ingredients together.

OPTION
You may substitute the pure vanilla bean paste for vanilla extract.

PECAN
COOKIES

MAKES 24 COOKIES

For those who like to sneak snacks into the movies like I do, you need these pecans in ya purse!

- 1/2 cup Earth balance, softened
- 1/2 cup granulated sugar
- 1/2 cup tightly packed brown sugar
- 1 egg
- 1 teaspoon pure vanilla bean paste
- 1 1/2 cups all purpose flour
- 1/2 teaspoon baking soda
- 1/4 teaspoon salt
- 1/2 cup chopped pecans

DIRECTIONS
1. Preheat oven to 350 F.
2. In a mixing bowl, with a hand mixer, combine Earth Balance, granulated sugar, and brown sugar until smooth.
3. Add the egg and beat it in thoroughly.
4. Using a spatula, stir in remaining ingredients.
5. Using a tablespoon, make balls and place onto parchment paper lined baking sheet. An ungreased baking sheet is fine too.
6. Bake 10 minutes in the oven, or until edges are nicely browned.
7. Remove from oven and serve.

OPTION
You may substitute the pure vanilla bean paste for vanilla extract.

SWEET POTATO
CAKE

MAKES 10 TO 12 SERVINGS

This moist cake with a creamy topping is a party waiting to happen. And who doesn't love a good party? FYI it's okay to have a party and not invite anyone else.

FOR THE CAKE

- 1 1/2 cups all purpose flour
- 1/2 cup granulated sugar
- 1/2 cup tightly packed brown sugar
- 1 teaspoon baking soda
- 1 teaspoon baking powder
- 1/4 teaspoon salt
- 1 teaspoon ground cinnamon
- 1/4 teaspoon nutmeg
- 1/2 cup Simple Truth unsweetened almond milk
- 1/2 cup melted Earth balance
- 2 large eggs
- 2 teaspoons pure vanilla bean paste
- 2 cups grated sweet potatoes

DIRECTIONS

1. Preheat oven to 350 degrees F.
2. Prepare 9x9 inch baking pan by lightly greasing and flouring the pan.
3. In a large bowl, using a spoon, combine all dry ingredients together.
4. In another mixing bowl, using a whisk, combine all wet ingredients together.
5. Using a hand mixer, combine wet ingredients into dry ingredients.
6. Using a spatula, stir in sweet potatoes until well combined.
7. Pour cake batter into prepared baking pan and bake 30 minutes.
8. Allow cake to cool in the pan for 20 minutes, then spread the sweet potato puree.
9. Allow cake to cool completely before covering with frosting.

FOR THE PURÉE

- 3 tablespoons Earth Balance
- 1 1/4 cups grated sweet potatoes, tightly packed
- 1/4 cup tightly packed brown sugar
- 1/2 teaspoon pure vanilla bean paste

DIRECTIONS

1. Add sweet potatoes to a saucepan. Fill saucepan with water so it covers the sweet potatoes. Boil on high heat for 15 minutes. Drain potatoes and add them to a mixing bowl.
2. Using a hand mixer, blend sweet potatoes until smooth.
3. In the same saucepan, cleaned, add sweet potato puree with remaining ingredients. Cook on medium-high heat for 5 minutes. Stir occasionally with a spatula. Place in a bowl and let cool.

FOR THE FROSTING

- 2 tablespoons Earth Balance
- 1 (8 ounce) container Trader Joe's vegan cream cheese
- 1/4 cup powdered sugar
- 1/2 teaspoon pure vanilla bean paste

DIRECTIONS

1. In a mixing bowl, with a hand mixer, combine Earth Balance and vegan cream cheese until creamy and lump-free.
2. Add powdered sugar and vanilla bean paste and stir with a spatula until well combined.
3. Refrigerate 1 hour.

TIP

Make your frosting first and refrigerate. While the cake is in the oven, make the purée.

OPTION

You may substitute the pure vanilla bean paste for vanilla extract.

Made in the
USA
Middletown, DE